❖❖❖❖

NIL DESPERANDUM
(Never Despair)

❖❖❖❖

POEMS BY SHARRON MURGATROYD

Illustrations by John Fuller

Published by

Romney Publications
Graseby House · Exning Road · Newmarket · Suffolk CB8 0AU

First published 1997

©Sharron Murgatroyd 1997

©This edition Romney Publications

ISBN 0 9528566 2 X

Designed and Typeset by
Equine Veterinary Journal Ltd

Printed by
Caligraving Ltd · Thetford · Norfolk · England

Cover designed by:
Richard Snowball

Front cover photograph:
Beechwood Cottage and Sharron
(Photograph by Fotosport (Racing))

Back cover photgraph:
Fiefdom and Sharron

✤✤✤✤

FOREWORD BY GRIFF RHYS JONES

This is Sharron Murgatroyd's second book. It's a collection of poems. Some were written when she was young, some more recently, but all of them overshadowed by the events of one day in Bangor in 1991 when Sharron fell from her horse. This was not unusual for Sharron. She was, after all, a jump jockey: a tough world of fences and races and spills. But, on that particular sunny afternoon, hers was no ordinary tumble, it left her paralysed. These poems were written in the face of a painful struggle with a crippling disability.

But wait a minute. Don't read these poems out of pity. Read them because there is another struggle here, and that is the struggle with hope and despair and dreams. Few can have faced up to it and sailed across it with such brave enthusiasm. In these poems she addresses subjects as personal as family breakdown and dashed expectations of a physical life she had once lived. She looks her helplessness squarely in the face and sees it for the phantom that it is. She seeks neither your pity nor your comfort, but opens up her heart and gives us something honest and good.

Of course I was moved by these poems. You will be too. There is such strength of will, such steadiness and such love. Welcome to the world of Sharron Murgatroyd. I hope, like me, you feel privileged to gain entrance.

✤✤✤✤

CONTENTS

✤✤✤✤

DEDICATION

*For my brothers **Clive** and **Mark**,*
*My sister **Justine**.*
And
***Bonita, Helen** and **David**.*
Nieces and Nephews
Kelly
Matthew
Alyshia
James
And twins
***Brodie** and **Jake**.*

A special thank you to:

***My Mother, Thelma,** who put in many hours of work helping me put this book together.*

***Ian McIntyre**, who had to put up with my endless queries on why I have to have a certain amount of structure within my poems. He explained with patience on our long sessions working through my often raw work, that although protocol can be broken, it hasn't to be ripped to shreds! I'm just a bit different with my style but I was willing to compromise and try hard to get it right. And no, I didn't want to be likened to McGonagall!*

***Ian Wallace**, who I now regard as my friend and mentor, for pointing me in the right direction and encouraging me by reading or having to listen to various poems over the telephone whether he wanted to or not...*

*Poet **Laurence Cotterell**, whose suggestions were sometimes adhered to and sometimes not but a great deal was learnt.*

***My ladies**, who had to become overnight secretaries, making notes, passing and turning over pages, finding pages, which were in such a secure place, that I couldn't remember where they were. As well as their other jobs.*

***Dr Peter Rossdale**, without whom my first book* "Jump Jockeys Don't Cry" *would never have been realised, thus leading to this second attempt.*

*All the **girls at EVJ** Publishers, I know you hide in the mail room while I'm on hold!*

***John Fuller**, for his wonderful illustrations.*

*And last but not least **Griff Rhys Jones** for writing the foreword.*

✤✤✤✤

✤✤✤✤

TEENAGE YEARS

1973–1979

✤✤✤✤

STREAKY RED SKY

The sky was a streaky red
I felt so happy
As I looked out of my bedroom window.
Then in a slow mysterious way
The sky became darkened
Big black clouds intermingled
With the red streaks of the sky.
The day was nearing its end
And the night was just beginning.

Then as if by magic
The black clouds disappeared
And once again the sky
Filled with a streaky red fire.
It looked like paint
Brushed daftly but delicately.
Smoke rose from a chimney near by
And helped to smother
The streaky red sky.

1973

THE STALLION

The slender legs of the racehorse moved swiftly.
His flowing mane and tail
Looked superb against the sunlit mountains
Suddenly he froze;
Reared and tightened his muscular body.
Veins of well bred horse could be seen
As I watched the four year old enjoying himself.

Next I noticed his eyes
Like fireballs moulded into his skull.
Black rimmed, red sparkling eyes
They reminded me of the first glow of sunlight
Through the morning mist.
His black silky coat shone in the first light of day
And a feeling of freedom
Came into my body.

1973

PAINTING

Moonlit sky spreads very wide
Stars smile at two lovers
Standing side by side.
The river's cool - the painting's blue
A silver stallion
And his love new.

Together they could gallop at top speed
Through the shallow stream.
Soft, smooth coats
Glisten in the atmosphere
That moves slowly round
For a brand new year.

1973

FRIENDSHIP

And when you lose someone near
Then you wish all the words
You wanted to say
Could have been clear.

And now the curtain has fallen
Over a friendship
We both wanted so much;
We taught each other to be free
To be so happy.

Now we've had to part
And I feel the ache
In my heart
He was like a brother
Not a lover.

WONDERING

As I look out over the land
I see the society of man.
It's Sunday ten past one
My hands are cold and feelings numb.
The wind is blowing my hair
But I don't care - I just don't care.

As I look to the east
I see the sun shining on me.
It's glow is cool
And I wonder how long it will be
Before the clouds intervene.

Bare trees surround me.
Small cottage sits on a far away hill
A lonely one but who can tell
What is beyond my sight;
It may be heaven,it maybe hell
It maybe love but who can tell?

Lonely is the figure that sits on the bench
Writing to who?
Freezing to the marrow.
And listening to the people in her head
Observing from North to South
From East and West.

1974

FINDING FREEDOM

Yesterday she woke reaching for you
But oh too soon she realised
You'd gone.
Out of our life
Out of our home
Into the future unknown.
So we have to bury our past
Along with the memory of you.

Running away we see your face
Running away from us;
Was it something we did
Or something that we said?

Out of the way it's a busy day.
No time to stop and say
Why you're leaving
Us all today,
For someone
Who has made you stray.
Money, wife, you causing strife
Your life, or are you finding freedom?

1975

YOU'RE THE REASON WHY

It's hard when you're nobody
It tears my soul to see you cry
And I know how much you love me
Even now I see pride glow in your eyes.
I won't do any wrong
You're the reason why.

You're the fight in me
Your voice swims round my head.
I'll show this world I'm somebody
You'll see in time
Sweet mother of mine
You're the reason why.

Good, bad and ugly
I'll see them all
You'll be proud of me.
All worry, stress and strain
Will soon leave your mind,
I'll wash away those tired lines.

I see you slowly giving in
Killing yourself to live
But please hold on
It won't be long
I'll make sure
You'll be the proud mum.

Life will no longer be hell
And when I get to my aim
I'll tell them all!
Sweet mother of mine
I'll tell them all!
You're the reason why.

1976

TODAY, TOMORROW OR THE NEXT DAY...

Seeing smiling pictures
Thinking about all I know
They teach us
And they preach to us
Even when we say no.

But when it comes to leaving
Signing papers no deceiving
You look back on your life
Wonder if you'll become a wife.
Not me! I say
I'm going to be someone today
Or maybe tomorrow
Or the next day.

The rest of my life is mine
I won't let it slip unsuccessfully by.
Goodbye Sir and Miss
I'll be back when I've
Made the movie list;
I'm going to be someone today
Or maybe tomorrow
Or the next day.

I've enjoyed my time at school
They tried to teach me
The golden rules.
I've been good
I've been bad
And I'll leave a little sad.

Then as I say my last goodbyes
I'll wipe a tear from my eye.
Walk into the second stage of life
With some knowledge
Maybe a little alone.

But remember I'll be back
When I've won the race.
I'm going to be someone today
Or maybe tomorrow
Or the next day.

1976

HORSES WERE MY FIRST LOVE

The light begins to fade
And darkness slowly creeps in.
I didn't know what I was looking for
But now as the clock ticks on
I know my decision isn't wrong.

Tomorrow; darkness my friend
Whom I have come to love
I start a new life
And I thank God above.

Horses were my first love
My future depends on them
Maybe I'll hurt people on the way
But in time I will repay.

To feel a racehorse between my knees
To feel him gallop on
To smell his odour
Which fills my mind;
He's big and strong.

Breaking the wire at the end
Is now my only dream
With time and patience on my hands
I'll ride "The Black";
Make him understand.

I'll love him, care and treat him well.
Triumphant I will ride
And see the pride in mother's eyes
When I thunder past the winning line.

1976

"BASALT"

Standing in your stable when everything is done
You shine
And it makes me feel
My life has really begun.
If only you knew the power you possess
Perhaps you'd leave us all.
The excitement I feel
When you gallop along
Makes me quite sure,
With you I belong.

Gentle giant;
I wish you were mine
We are great friends
And I know my heart will break,
When it comes to the time
That we have to say
Goodbye.

1976

"LEYBURN LADY"

The stable yard is quiet
Only soft munching
Can be heard
Everywhere's neat and tidy
No straw by the door.

But you stand out from all the rest
Big bright eyes
Peer out from a chestnut face
Four white socks and a long white blaze
Leyburn Lady full of grace.

When you first came
You were lonely and afraid
Looking out of your stable door
Asking questions; with face to the floor.

Now you've settled in and life is good once more
Just like me in every way
The first steps are hard
But easy with each day.

1976

RECALL AND LEAVE

Listening for a voice
To come through the stillness of the night,
I lie awake in my bed
Not even the moon is bright.
Familiarities all around
Escape only to be found.
Eager to find where I belong
The way is long
Must be strong.

Thinking of someone
Who has gone before
Needing someone to share
This heavy load.

Waking, reaching for yesterday
Remorse is something I have seen
In its clutches I have been
Only to find solitude.
Unseen faces of an unseen breed.
Listen to the creepiness of a windy night.

Years have flown
We have grown
Just one more quick glance
Stop! listen for that voice.
Wish it peace, dream of it and see
But please
Just let it be.

1976

FOUNDATION TRUTHS

And had the word been given before
Maybe we would cry no more
Realisation of the human race
Offered a remedy
No one could take,
So all denying brought dissatisfaction.
I have often asked myself
The reason for the saddened universe
Where crying is a lullaby.

See the tapestry of ignoble children
Looking for a shadow, red or gold
Looking for wisdom unknown.
Sweet tasting good life
So uneasily found.
Take the remedy or leave
For there is no bargaining
With red or gold
No bargaining with
The dark shadows of death.

1976

TRAGEDY OF A FRIEND

The great day came
All nerves and tension worked the morning time.
I stayed at home
But wished I was there,
To see you walk round in the National parade.
Intelligent eyes beam from your head
You know why you're here
You heard it said.

On the television you looked so good
Aintree was in your blood
The big stiff fences loomed ahead
But nervousness never entered your head;
Cool and calm
This is your game
No other horse will be the same.

Is it a death trap?
Should it be allowed?
I can't make up my mind
I can't make a sound.
Would I ride in it if I could?
Yes! I think I really would.

The sun shone bright
The tape went up
Forty four runners all bunched up;
Disaster at the first horses fall down
Jockeys are hurt
But the crowd just looks round.

You had never fallen
In the whole of your career
You were going strong
There was no fear,
Except for loose horses that were there
This time Becher's
But you never made The Chair...

Tipping the top of the fence
It brought you rapidly down.
Falling on your neck
And then dead you lay
On the thundering ground.

No pain or agony or feeling of hurt,
Except for us who felt torn apart
And now it is too late.
Grand National day is gone
One horse made history
But the tragedy of our friend lives on.
The end of your day
Had fatally come,
Now only time can heal the pain
Of Becher's Brook
And
"Winter Rain".

1977

ONLY LOVERS

I ache for you
From deep within
I try but where do I begin
Alone again;
And silence seems to be
A feeling of forgotten means.

I ache for you
When I'm in my bed
And the day's events swim round my head
Flickering flames of an unlit fire
I see you
And I'm filled with desire.

I ache for you
But to you it doesn't matter
You love me now
And tomorrow everything scatters
Picking up broken pieces
Of nothing that has fallen.
You don't know
How I ache
How I have been stolen.

I ache for a friend
Not just a lover now
But we hardly ever speak
When we are together
We hardly ever speak
Sometimes never.

I ache for those strong words
That are spoken
But only by others
Nothing is held between us
We are only lovers.

I ache for you
While I light a cigarette
I think of situations
Where do I go?
Where do I wait?
A pain stabs sharp
You've left me in the dark.

I ache for you
But now you've gone
And things I should have said
Are forgotten;
Were they wrong?
In a sun filtered forest
I walk alone
Where I wished for something
I thought could be strong.

1977

SANCTUARY

Reflections play on a stream
As the darkness deepens
Slowly to rise into day.
A bird swoops down and gives a cry
Then the brilliant sun shines rich and bold
I ask anything to be foretold
But only silence breaks through
My soul.

Big trees sway
As their shadows dance and play
And I can hear music
Sounds of laughter everywhere.
An authoritative hand
Was the ghost of a man
Raged then invisible
A blinkered eye as tears arrive.
Why did they ask questions - why?

Reaching out for an unborn bud
Naturally growing in all serenity and love.
Clinging onto a feeling
As furtive hands try to hold
Something that is not mine.
And a bird swoops down and gives a cry
I ask anything to be foretold
But only silence breaks through
My soul.

✤✤✤✤

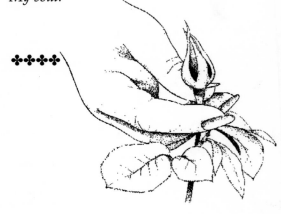

1977

I FELT LIKE A WOMAN

I felt like a woman last night
I felt like a woman when you came to me
And smothered us with something you can't see;
Something we can't be.
Then why in the night are you so clear
Yet by day so unreal.

And I know

You felt like a man last night
You felt like a man when I came to you
And I gave you my everything
Even though we can never be seen
But one day maybe; maybe.

And you know

It's too late to call you
At this hour of the day
But I just wanted to say
Wanted to say
I love you.

1978

LISTEN TO THE CARDS

The harmony based on my own satisfaction
Gave me a feeling
To look at the beauty that surrounded you.

A powerful person
But so easily am I neutralised
By your physical strength
That effaced me.

Then he came, tried to love me.
Too weak.
I can be a tower of destruction
Unavoidable disaster
Like he found out.
I'm sorry for him - my love gone
But you have taken my soul away.

The moon tried to tell him my meaning
I am illusion
And the sun tried to tell him
Triumph is slightly delayed
But never in my mind destroyed.

But the thought of you won't go away
I don't want you to be my triumph
I want to love him
I can believe in him
Someone to trust
But you have left nothing in me
No love; not even a trace of lust.

1978

WEEPING WALLS

Look into that window
Tell me what you see
Nothing except a weeping wall
That's me:
Feeling lonely once again
When will torment finally end
One after another I can't go on
A weeping wall that never began.

Waiting always waiting
In pathetic anticipation
Don't know where I'm going to;
Don't know where I've been
Restless nights full of confusing dreams
With weeping walls closing in on me.

Coldness of the bare floor
Relentless to my heels
Long blue shadows traced
Stretching across the ceiling
From beam to beam
Touch the colours black and grey
Why do I hide behind penetrating eyes
Weeping walls - my disguise.

Take your place
Step into a desolation row
Wanting always a little more.
Now delusion has slowly set in
Loneliness creeping up from within.
A weeping wall appears
Tall, cold and thin.

Play the music loud and shut out the light
Keeping me from the crowd
Perils and monsters dressed in black
Keep me from harm
Tell me I'm strong
Weeping walls to you I belong.

1978

FACE TO FACE

I recognise the picture
Framed beautiful and sweet
Always a carefree face
In the delicate night's heat.
Wandering around laughing
Sometimes curt,
But I've seen that face
Screwed up in pain and hurt
Then untwined as if suddenly
It's seen a new light.

Deep feeling eyes
For everyone around
Lips so fine like a stem
Of a proudly grown vine.
Nobody wants to be tied
Even though it is so full of caring,
Blooming free
For everyone to see.

Flowers and fruits open their eyes
When the face walks by
In an array of amazement.
The sun shines down its rays,
With pictures all untrue.
The mystery remains unsolved
Until the days rise again
And the blue bird sings
Will the face be free
To fly her word on a wing?

1978

SLEEPY LAGOON

Feeling not so good inside
Unhappiness makes me have tired lines
I lie back and try to visualise
A face in the mirror
Without sad eyes.
But instead I'll take a look at the moon
And slide on down to the
Sleepy Lagoon.

I walk down desolate streets
But there I find no peace.
Looking for reasons right
But tears drown my thoughts
Then a shiver runs me cold
As I see in the reflection of the moon
A girl sliding on down to the
Sleepy Lagoon.

One day someone will share my dream
By day the sun
Shines down on the sea.
I'll walk you on the path it has made for me
Towards the shore that stretches
With ever endless golden sand.
Then by night
I'll see another reflection
In the light of the moon
As we gently slide on down to the
Sleepy Lagoon.

1979

"BROTHER BRONCHO"

A partnership based on
Understanding and trust
That's what we have both of us
And when I need to talk
I know where to go
To my best friend Brother Broncho.

Jet black coat that I brush 'till it shines
A big white blaze and a funny
Black and white eye.
Every day you wait for me;
Head over the stable door
Saying hello with a whickering call.

Then in the racecourse paddock
You hold your head up high
Sometimes prancing with excitement
Feeling good inside.
And you try to bite me as girth pulls tight
You know you are here
To race and fight.

And I wait anxiously while the race is on
Please God don't let him put a foot wrong
A fatal fall is what I dread
I couldn't bear to see you badly hurt then dead.

Over the last and there's a clap and cheer
You know you've won
And I feel proud to be here.
A pat, a hug I hope you know
You're my best friend
Brother Broncho.

1979

RACING DAY WAIT

How many times did we pass by
Before we met
Before I realised
That you were going to be a friend of mine?

And now when we see each other
It's only for a shortwhile,
Exchange of a few words
A few smiles, we laugh but never frown.
Let's have a game - three card brag
I bet my racehorse
Can beat your old nag!

Then once in a cold morning
We walked and talked
As the sea blew in sand and salt
And the wind carried our laughter away
As we held hands on that cold and biting
Racing day.

I wish we had more time to share
Now I've realised - I want to care
But the wind carries my voice away
And I'll have to wait for another
Racing day.

1979

REJECTED LOVE: FREEDOM IS FINE.

Drove to a place
Where I hadn't been for a while
A place where the laughter
Nourished my body in the summer sky
Seeing the old faces again
Smiling hellos - friends
Summer friends of old.

Then turning round I caught sight
Of a half lit face in the disco light
Trembling - a small feeling
A lost ache of the past - an ache
That should never have been allowed to last.

Then all of a sudden the place went dark
A whirl of mystic as we smiled.
Uprising feeling - alive again
In the place deep inside
Where once I was marked.
How did we end up here
Together again after all these years?

Holding on to each other
Like nothing else mattered.
Reminiscing about comic verse
We laughed and cried
Even though the song was never mine.
And the peaceful waters flowed
While the hours we shared glowed.

Time swept away
And we were revealed in the wicked light
Of a very different day.
The white sheets have faded now
Discoloured:
As we both realise we can never
Love each other.

I drive you home - leave you there
The scent of one kiss left hanging
In the air.
So soon to turn me cold
As the urgent touch fades
Returning to my senses
And my own life I've made

1979

"I'M A DRIVER"
(WAS SPEEDING)

"Driver was speeding" - they said today
Another record broken
On another racing day
They said he jumped higher - higher than ever today
I was so proud of him as
He led all the way.

And I'll remember forever
Those days spent together
From the very first small race
To the biggest one ever.
Ascot - Cheltenham
Here we come and at Ascot we raced
And at Ascot we won.

I can still feel that knot deep down inside
A frightening feeling
I never could hide
I could hardly watch
I could hardly look
As you flew towards the open ditch
You must jump "Driver"
You're going too quick!

I'll never forget the glory we had
Record breaking triumphs
With your bold jumping nerve.
The whispers of the public as we walked round
And both of us feeling
So damn proud.

Then in your stable you were so calm
A long way away from your excited state
Of the racecourse blare.
So relaxed you liked me to
Brush your face and cuddle you.
"Driver was speeding"
They said today
Another record broken - on another racing day.

1979

AMBITION AND LOVE

1980–1991

"GYMER"

Gone forever
Now gone; but not forgotten
I wish so much that you could stay.
A real partnership was made
Waiting for those
Winter racing days.

But the rich men
You know what they say
They have to spoil everything
And sell you away.

Face to face
With my horse my Gyme
Big white blaze and ever searching eyes.
That silent understanding
Now so quickly dies
Racing over flights
It feels so good
It feels so right
It happened in my dream
Last night.

The stable yard is quiet
Only soft munching can be heard.
But turning round
I see your head over the stable door
It seems for so long
Then as I take a step to see
I realise it's not you
Because my Gyme you've gone.

THIS NEED OF MINE

How long I waited
For this time of year
After long summer days
The Winter is here.
Sharp, fresh mornings
Gripping me
A feeling of freedom
My freedom - I see.

Racing days seem so long
While I keep waiting
Standing aside just watching
Heart just aching
For my need is as yours
But while you're
Race riding
I'm stood in pause.

The winners' enclosure
Somewhere you've been
Not for so long
For me I've only seen.
A jockey's life
Sometimes a joke
For the thing in the
Two-thirty is "one big yoke."

But the winners
Will soon roll on in
Then my chance will come
And I'll be able to race ride
Some hurdlers we've got
And the odd fall
Or two
Will be forgot.

Then Winter nights will glow
And I'll feel content
Not so low
The dreams will have all gone
Replaced by things
We wished for
And I hope this will
Happen for you
Because I know you need it too.

And I hope we will
Still be friends
Even though we'll be rivals
In the end.
Because this need of mine
Is so strong
Even if it means
In a man's world
I belong.

BUT YOU...

The stars shone and twinkled
My arms held you close
And I was so frightened
In case you were a ghost.
As I tried to sleep
I kept seeing you smiling at me
And I wondered how this could be.

Even though

I need you to hold me
But you don't;
I need you to want me
But you won't;
I need you to love me
But you can't.

So now when I see you
I'll try to ignore you, pretend
Dinner is off tonight
If I can't have all of you
It wouldn't be right.
So in your car then gone
And I'll have to find an excuse
Why it's so wrong.

Because

You need to hold me
But you don't;
You need to want me
But you won't;
You need to love me
But you can't.

So we'll just remain
The friends we've been
We'll laugh and joke
Openly seen
But never can we meet alone there
For we can't risk showing
How much we care.

And you know

We need to hold
But we don't;
We need to want
But we won't;
We need to love too
And it could hurt
If we find that we do.

IF I CAN...

If I can make you cry
If I can fill your eyes with pleasure
Just by holding you;
Well that's enough for me
But if you don't really care
Then let me be.

If I can make you smile
When the day's been long
And you feel so tired
'cause the winners have passed you by;
Well that's enough for me
If we share a little time
Then let us be.

If I can make you love
If I can still find a comfort
In my waiting for you
As the days slowly drift on by
Your promise kept
But now I suppose this is goodbye.

Well that's enough for me
If only friends you want to be.
But I'll still think of you and me
You and I;
How our pleasure makes me cry.

IT'S NOT FAIR !

It's not fair
When you say - I can
Then you say - I can't.
It's not fair
When you say - I'll get hurt
You say for a girl
It's just too rough!
Well if I get hurt
Then that's just tough.

It's not fair
When I work so hard
To live my dream
And I wait and wait.
It's not fair - you know
For now I could scream.

It's not fair
'cause now I feel useless
Not good enough to even try.
It's not fair
When that lump in my throat
Almost makes me cry.

It's not fair
'cause I'm a girl
In a world made for men,
It won't be fair until
I race ride over jumps
and
Ride over jumps I will!

47

A HAND IN MINE

It seemed really strange
You being here
Only for a short while
But the moment's so dear.
A fleeting visit
For us to find;
A hand in yours
And
A hand in mine.

For weekdays are spent alone
Screaming - loving - forlorn
And our moments are so dear,
I hold them close
Hold you near
Now I'd like to find;
A hand in yours
And
A hand in mine.

All our yesterdays
Are still to come
But now I'm tired
The night has begun.
And the moment of you
Lingers on
But I'll have to wait
Another day
Before I find
A hand in yours
And
A hand in mine.

❖❖❖❖

THUNDERING HOOVES

And the man stood by her side
Hand on shoulder - love he could not hide.
The air felt good on her arms and face;
Vaguely recognising its taste.
As if the outdoor life was hers
Confused - sometimes
She shivered in the wheelchair...

She tried to remember the faces
As they walked by - smiling sweetly
But she didn't know why.
Quite embarrassed they were, she knew
For here she was
Locked in a silent hue.

The people they talked, she tried to make sense
She sat with a stare sometimes
Wrenching his heart.
Late into the night she lay sleepless
Vague thoughts tried to break through;
Thundering hooves - always - thundering hooves.
In a nightmare fright she'd hear him cry
"Oh God why? Oh my God! - why...?"

A shimmer of sunlight caught her eye,
Her sudden movement made every one look.
For a moment she seemed to recognise;
But as a glimpse does fade
Then the hope did die.

The times he hugged her - but no joy she knew
Numbed by the crashing fall;
Thundering hooves - always - thundering hooves
She'd just look and stare
And he would weep for her
As she sat in her wheelchair.

As if with pleasure the soft muzzle
Touched her hand.
She felt it warm - she stirred inside
A message to say she was still alive!
A smile; the first since that dreadful day
Passed over her face in a lightening way
And the sheer joy he felt pass through
Was enough to break
Her silent hue.

19 YEARS AGO
AUGUST '70

So nineteen years later
We all sit here
We've been through the dirtwater
Mum the boys and me,
And what of poor Justine
She was only three!

So nineteen years have passed my door
And what have we all found out?
We found that we could manage Mr.
With you or without.

Nineteen years for Mother
That's what grieves me most.
Nothing has been done
To try to ease her pain.
There must be someone out there
Someone else to blame.

Nineteen years of weeping
Sobbing from a heart
Half a lifetime lost of love
A lifetime torn apart.

Was that August warm
Nineteen years ago?
I seem to remember
A bright day that ended with a storm
I remember fun and laughter
Then tears through 'till morn.

Then I remember dirtwater
Mother pulled us through
It clung to us like stink...
One parent families - Like glue
Dirtwater they called it
That's what made us feel so low
Nineteen years ago.

I honestly thought you loved us
But I was proved wrong
Even though you left us
You could have loved us strong.

No worry all hurry
Your family's down in dirtwater
"No not mine
I haven't got a family
I'm busy all the time!"

I hope my man he loves me
I hope my man is man
I hope he doesn't leave me
In dirtwater - I know he never can.

For now we are all strong you see
Strengthened by a blow
It started a long time back;
About nineteen years ago.

ROSES THAT YOU GAVE ME...

The roses that you picked for me
Have withered a little now
The roses that you gave me
So special for me now.
For it seems like forever
Since you went away
So I'll keep the roses in their vase
And hope their scent will stay.

The roses that you gave me
Came from our garden then
And they were all different colours
From the stem.
And like our love does blossom
The roses they do grow.
I was going to change them yesterday
But left them one day more.

So while you're away so many things to do
But every spare moment
I look to the skies and think of you.
So many miles away
I hope you are safe too.

The roses that you gave me
Forever for me to hold
The rose that tells me something
Never to be sold.
I wait for your return
In sunlight from your voyage
To tell me tales of travelling light
And love me for all time.

The roses that you gave me
Will wait in life I'm sure
So you can smell their sweet scent
As you walk in the door.
Laden with shades of different
Scents from across the sea.
A strong embrace to last for long
No urging to be free.

And while our love did glow that night
The roses bloomed free
So happy I am now that safe
You've returned to me.

THANKING YOU AT CHRISTMAS

Thanking you at Christmas - for the life
I've found;
Thanking you at Christmas - for the strength
Deep within,
Thanking you, my Mother, for you have kept me
from giving in.

And I didn't even realise, with the harsh words I spoke - how I hurt
you so - but I was hurting, tearing inside, suffering with my
broken heart - Oh sweet Mother of mine, you with never a word unkind
Stood there by my side, waiting for me to turn, someone there to find.

Thanking you at Christmas - for being
My friend;
Thanking you at Christmas - for it is now
I feel so alone.
Thanking you, my Mother, for you have pulled me through
And let me see another Christmas so white, so warm, so new.

Then one night, in quiet of dark, I asked the Lord to take me - away
from my broken heart - from all this pain take my soul - put it safe
away - let me come in heaven's door, then my suffering will be no more.

Thanking you at Christmas - for the Lord
He turned me away.
He said, "Your mother's holding you so near, you cannot
Enter here."
Thanking you at Christmas - with arms
Ever stretching out - stretching out for me.

Thanking you for Christmas - my Mother
My guiding light;
Thanking you for your words - I can hear in the long
And lonely night.
Thanking you at Christmas - forever in your debt
And soon the tears will all run dry - the tears that I have wept
The tears that you have tried to help me to forget.

LEAVE HIM BE

I thought it would last forever
Every night I'd say
Please bring him home to me
All my life to stay.
But then a voice in my dream
Said to me
"Let him go - love - leave him be.
For if you love him like you say
You can love him in a different
Kind of way.
And if that should be from afar
He'll feel it more for he too has a scar
So now I tell you in your dreams
Let him go - love - leave him be.
Home is not the place for him
If unhappiness leads to sin
And if you love him
Like you say
Then how could you make him stay.
Whilst he wanders lost for now
I'll keep him safe with me
So now I tell you in your dreams
Let him go - love - leave him be."

A LOVE TO WAIT...

Lay a hand upon my breast
And on my navel too.
You kiss my hands and kiss
My face - and say,
I'll wait for you.
I'll wait until the sun goes down
And skies of hope are blue.
I'll stroke your lovely curly hair
While I wait for you.

It may be long before I'm strong
Enough to show you love.
You lie patiently holding onto me
Waiting to be loved.
The ghost he stands just out of sight
By the door watching on
Even though he said - for me
His love had now all gone.

Lay a hand upon my breast
And on my navel too.
Stroke my brown curly hair
And say "I love you".
Kiss my face and smile at me
Kiss my face and hands.
I'll wait for you as long as it takes
I'll wait for you to land.

I'll hold you long into the night
Hug you when you're blue.
I'll wipe the tears from your face
When the ghost has frightened you.
Then one day we'll push him away
And you will hold on to me.
I'll feel your body next to mine
Our love will be brand new.

I'll lay a hand upon your breast
And on your navel too.
And you will want me more than love

For I will wait for you.
I'll wait for your heart to mend
With smiling in my eyes.
We'll lay so close that the ghost
Will not be able to divide.

I'll kiss your hands, kiss your face
Hold your aching limbs.
I'll stroke your lovely curly hair;
For one day as I wait
Your love will come to me.
A love that I have waited for
My love - when you want me.

FEEL

Feel like you're drowning
In the sea
And only so long can you fight
To be free.
Swirling waters drag you down
Your arms ache - body's weak
Then another breath you've found.

You think your passage has been rough
So far
Now you've lost your love.
Thrown in the big black sea
Now to feel the life that's real.
Cold dark waters drag you down
Feel like drowning
Then another breath you've found.

Some will survive the stormy sea
Some will just let go and be
Taken down in cold murky waters.
For no one knows - from one day on
The depths of the sea
How it is so strong.
Sometimes you're floating towards the shore
Then surging waters drag you back,
To your knees
And where you were before.

Cold waters embrace your shoulders
Trying to be a friend
But there is no warmth
Just a perilous end.
Swim to the shore
Through surging waters wade
For life is worth its weight in gold
A weight worthy of being saved.

EYES MEET...

Did our eyes meet - like the old cliche - across the crowded room,
Were you looking at me
As I glanced up at you?
You didn't look away with your stare
As I saw you standing there;
In the fleeting moment - long.
Did you see me in my loneliness
Looking forlorn?
Is there something for us to say
Or will the moment fade away?
Why did our eyes meet across the crowded room
Why did you look at me
And
Why did I hold my stare on you
In a fleeting moment - long?

ROMANCING AGAIN

Can the romancing start again
With dancing in my eyes?
So much to offer I have I've found
A love I cannot hide.
Will I ever be allowed to love
The love I have lost
Or will I have to romance with a bright new
Honey floss?

Can the romancing start again
With a stare from far away?
In those eyes the gleam
That says
"For now, I haven't even tried."
And
When I reach out for past love
But he just walks away.
Can
I turn and look at you
And will you still want me to stay?

Can the romancing start again
With a stare from a day old?
Someone to take my love so precious
For him to hold.
A stare that says romance for me
That came from a long lost day;
A stare that said romance with me when I was
Too blind to see.

PUT ON A SHOW

Glittering - Sparkling letting me know - That your life is just a show - How to look sometimes I wonder why - Then make an effort - Have some pride - Even if you feel like dying inside - Always make the time to please - If not yourself - Then think of me - People notice a lot of things - And if you're dowdy, feeling blue - They won't want to talk with you - So if you're blue put on a show - Let people notice where you go - Appearance says a lot for you - Say "Hello how are you" - Let the sparkle you have in your eyes - Dance and play in flickering candlelight - When someone takes you out tonight.

THE LADY IN WAITING

Here stands the lady in waiting
Waiting for the tide to turn.
For winter snows to go
The chill wind
That freezes her face
To gently blow over warm.

Here stands the lady in waiting
Forever now so alone.
As she looks across the land
Wondering if the hurt will ever go
If he will ever return
To take her hand.

Here stands the lady in waiting
Sad eyed now; the roses
Have withered and died
But the wretched sorrow
And pain of love
Still remains inside.

Here stands the lady in waiting
Staring out across the vortex sea
Balancing on the edge of life
Now no one can help her
Not even me.

For all the memories in her head
Driving a force of torment.
Is there a difference
Between life and death?
The lady is waiting to see.

COMFORTING IN ARMS

Sit here on the sofa
You hold me in your arms
You wrap me warm
And I hold you
In silence
Each comforting in arms.

And while at peace
In moments still
You're probably thinking of her
And I of him
But whilst in broken heart
Inside we still weep,
We may fall into sleep
Each comforting in arms.

A look - a smile
But no kiss for now
Just huggled together as if underground.
A hug that's warm for us to know
Always for now a place to go
To find some peace.
In darkened nights... safe
Each comforting in arms.

And while in truth
We both have now
In long distant past
They'll cry out loud.
No need to be lovers to find
Some peace
For both now we may sleep
Each comforting in arms.

STRANGERS NOW
AND
STRANGER STILL

Strangers now with only ordinary words to say - Everyday sayings when we meet pass our way - Strangers now and stranger still the way you look and act at will - For your decision at destiny end - Your desire to end my friend - My stranger now - I wait to care - Want to mend you - Stroke your hair - Love you like you loved me - But strangers now and stranger still - I wait contented in the wings - Looking on but leaving you - For that is all you want me to do - And that is all you'll let me give to you - Strangers now in days we meet - Exchange the pleasantries - Say with ease - And a smile - But still so deep - For stranger still -Is how we act - Not wanting each other to hurt - Even though sometimes curt - Then regret -But in my loneliness - Never strangers in my night - I think of you and know my love was right - So by day we're strangers now - But never can we be strangers still - For the home I'm living in - Keeping warm - And stranger still - Waiting for the stranger - Only if at his own will - Never for me - Stranger still...

BROKEN HEARTED DAUGHTERS

Oh my Lord above, what have I done so wrong?
For you to make me endure
This pain - to last - my life - so long.
After years of aching heart I thought at last
In my later years I would relax;
Always a memory of him every day
In my childrens' faces, in what they say
But soothing calm would come my way.
Now I find my heart he slaughters
I live again
With my broken hearted daughters.

Within a year from wedding bed
My only love to leave he fled
From one affair unto another, leaving me
His wife - to suffer.
And now the first born daughter's here
Like no other her sweet baby face so clear
And in her innocence she never knew
Why mother held her tight in the middle of the night.
Her husband now to love her strong
Her husband now to tell no lies
But baby cried as hot tears fell on her
From her mother's eyes.
Please never to put her through
My heart he slaughters
But now I live again
With my broken hearted daughters.

Oh tried I did, my heart to mend
I fought for him to be my friend
I prayed at night to God above
Please make him return - my special love.
For all my life some happiness and peace
So God gave me another daughter
Some sort of relief,
And as we smiled down on her that day
May I forgive him for now to never go away.
Two beautiful daughters will make him stay.
But Oh! For him to still put me through
My life and heart he slaughters
As I have to again feel
With my broken hearted daughters.

In their childhood everyday I'd pray
For happiness to come their way
Hope they'd meet the man of their dreams
To keep them safe, marry them - all their life to be.
Never have to feel the pain
Of man unfaithful - driving me insane.
And as I watch them in their play
They would look up and say "why did daddy go away?
But it's alright, Mummy, for we love you
And know forever you will stay."
That's what helped me, live for them, each cold day.
But my fear now is here
I feel their pain;
My heart he slaughters, again and again
With my broken hearted daughters.

And why, God, have You put them through
This pain and agony that I have too?
Did I ask too much?
Is that why You deny us of love's forever touch?
Every day of my life
I've tried to find a reason why - why
He left me, his wife, with all the treasures
We made in our strife?
Now I know myself am safe
For ebbed away has longing for any man's
Love or taste.
But what of my two beautiful daughters?
Will forever they have to live
My life of heart's torture.
So young, and lively in their eyes, I see
And wonder why their men they loved so much
Could ever leave
Their loving hearts to slaughter
For the pain now in their eyes
My broken hearted daughters.

If only now You could send
Some love and happiness their hearts to mend,
With friend and lover for them to hold
Forever this their precious love never to be sold.
For now I cannot bear to see such wanton slaughter
Now alone; I have to watch
My broken hearted daughters.

PLATONIC AFFAIR

Hello! ... My friend, did you say
That maybe we could drift away
Together for a few peaceful days
Hiding from my busy life
From my troubles and my strife.
Quiet to sit amidst some silent thoughts
Each of us so special to share
Some happiness in our...
Platonic Affair

Far away across the sea
They won't know where to look for me,
But I'll be safe beneath your wings
My friend...
Lending me a hand to hold
A shoulder to rest my weary soul
And I know that you won't mind... if
In your safe hug I weep a little more
Into the sea... into the floods
For each of us so special to share
We'll find some happiness in our...
Platonic Affair.

I know that you will understand
As you hold me close... so delicate I am
A friend to share the moonlight's trail.
We'll sit through to watch the rising sun
Almost forgetting yesterday's tears.
You'll gently tread away... after kissing me
Goodnight
As we sleep... so special to share
Is our happiness in our...
Platonic affair.

DID I... DID YOU... DID WE...?

*Did we... arrange to meet
In secret one night in the week.
Did they... all see us there too
Not knowing you were meeting me and I was meeting you.
Did we... say hello with gentle kiss
Friends for long
Nothing seemingly amiss?*

*Did I... wander round umbrella taut against the wind and rain
A secret smile as we caught a glance
Knowing soon we would be talking
Like friends do.
Did we... laugh and chatter long into the night
Trying to put everything right.
And once or twice as you drove
Did you... look into my face and
Did I... shyly look away
Even though we are only friends today?*

*Did we... both feel so at ease to say and do as we please
Was it comfortable for you to know
Always a warm place for you to go.
Did I... share my secrets too
My secrets that no one else knew
Did you... look on quite surprised, impressed
Then sort of sad-eyed?
Then in your tiredness that I saw
I put away the book
And we turned to different bedroom doors.*

*Did I... thank you for lovely night
A fleeting kiss that felt just right.
Did we... say no more today
For maybe that's to be the way
Did you... sort of show some love
In secret as we talked.
Did we... ever dream a dream
A lover to come for you and me.
Or will we just pass the time of day
In our lovely friendly way?*

HOW CAN WE BE FRIENDS?

Now you ask me to be your friend
After all these endless years;
Our loving hearts that cannot mend
When they have been so badly torn.
Now you hold out your hand - too late... to see
For where was the comforting hold
From a daddy... that should have been for me?
When life took it's toughest toll
When people hurt us so
They're not what they seem... where were you
When we were in need?

Now you ask me to be your friend
Maybe for the last time - no softness
In your eyes, just same old arrogant voice.
New life without us you made - it was you
Who had the choice...
And in moments dear, to look into my Mother's eyes
The pain of years in her sacrifice
From the moment she had to let you go
The burden of heartache now and forever
To rest in her soul.
When in times we cried out... "We need you so!"
But how can we be friends... when in darkness
You turned face - wavered your head - just saying no
Then drove away forever out of Coley Road.

Now you ask me to be your friend,
But you'll never know me
No love to send...
You don't know my lucky colours
Or triumphs that I've made.
You don't know where I live - or food I taste
You don't even know what I like,
Or if I nearly died in bed - one cold and lonely night
When, through my own heartache, I again had to look
To my Mother for only God knows - the only one to care
Now kneeling I thank her, someone always to be there.

So, how can we be friends now...
After all these years?
When I have been a witness to... oh so many tears,
So long to live our lives alone.
I understand you had to go
But to leave us telling lies
Words to haunt me as the years go by.
Not even asking if we were safe - if we were warm
Had we managed fatherless... weathering the storm?
Father leaving children and wife
Fleeing to lover in the night!

And as you turned to go away
The babies you made in your love
Were only faint voices, in the dark
Long lost voices, in a cradling hold
Five tiny voices that cried out loud
How we loved you so... as a piece of us died
When on our lives - you turned and closed the door.

So, how can we be friends... now?
No effort have you made,
You've let the years flow by - happy with your way
Never to be a friend - or father
And I am just a stranger... standing in the shade.
In my heartache I'll always feel
I'm lucky to have someone... forever to be real:
Someone who has always been
Mother... father... and friend to me.

❖❖❖❖

WHO DARES... WINS!

I hide away
Sorry and crying out for yesterday
Leave me wretched in my pain
Never ever to love again.
I fought for you in years gone by
Tried to reach out and bring you the sky
But now you don't want to speak to me
With eyes to the floor.
Plain and simple you don't want me anymore.

Something deep inside
Shook me hard saying I had to try
Even when I argued why.
Hard times held my hand at bay
Even with the wicked things that people say.
But now with head held very high
After friendly voice did prompt me,
To be brave and change my darkened life.
To ask for something is not a sin
Then you will know that;
Who dares wins!

TUNNEL VISION

Time is the long ago
And in my life
Lay things I did not want to know:
I had my love
I had my home
Tunnel Vision
Nowhere else to go.
My love!
The brightest thing
Ever to happen to me;
Oh for the life in each other
We distilled.
The laughter in our home we built
Doomed, like a house of cards, to fold.
My love
My precious love
You sold.

Then, in my Tunnel Vision,
In darkness
I was left alone.
Tunnel Vision
Now I had to make it on my own.
Days were dark as the night
No-one to love me
Or hold me tight.
I had to break-out
And fight!
From the Tunnel Vision
That surrounded me
When I was in protected love
So safe;
Eternity for you and me.
I've had to find a different life
Alone now
But not for many more nights.

I've had to tread
Such a different path.
New life I've found
Tunnel Vision could not last
I could not keep us
Living in the past;

In Tunnel Vision
I could no longer survive,
For when my love said goodbye
The tunnel filled with water
So near to death was I
I had to fight to surface
I had to be strong.
Break the ties... from the tunnel
My sole vision for so long:
Then slowly and, at times, disguised,
I opened and dried
My saddened eyes.
Walked out of my small, dark tunnel
Into a bigger, bluer, sunnier sky.

IS IT FATE?

Is it fate... that brought you here
Saying hello, feeling no fear?
Smiling eyes I have not seen
Since broken-hearted I have been.
Did our eyes look so deep?
Searching I am, but only in my sleep.

At ease I am now... at ease
For it will be left only to my fate
If you are to need me.
Relaxed and smiling sort of nothing
But was there something in our smiles?
Telling us one thing... is it fate?
Then casually saying goodnight
Friendly kisses cheek to cheek
Maybe see you again?
Yes, you say, I'm sure you will.
I drive away slightly confused
What's my fate... is it you!
Morning light... I try to picture you
I can hardly remember your face last night.
Your vision has vanished away... is it fate?

Will I ever see you again
Is it fate... and if so when?
Days and nights are long
Got to be so very strong.
I see you bungling down my hall
Is it fate... or are you there at all?

A DIFFERENT KIND OF LIFE

1991–1997

WHAT CAN YOU SAY?

What can you say to me now?
You see me
Then you have to look away:
In your memory
You can still see me dance
Your hazel eyes flickering gently over my smiling face
Our eyes played and flirted
Just a little that warm, sunny day
Waiting for a special time
Never now... and

What can we say ?

You look at me,
I'm just the same
Except the dance that's gone away:
I sit still I cannot move
No hands or arms to embrace you
So sad the blue and hazel eyes no more flirting
In sunny skies:
But you can hold me in my dreams
In the day or night
I can still smile and laugh... so

What can you say ?

THE SHADOW

I feel a presence around me now
Watching me whilst I sit in my home,
Thinking or hoping that I don't know,
But I can feel and I can see.
I know the shadow is watching me
Walking slowly over the land
Looking for lost treasures,
Then stealing with a furtive hand
Secretly tip-toeing by the windows
And startled to find
I nearly saw him out of the corner of my eye.

Cold night falls again and shadow tries to slip
In my door,
Always hiding maybe forever more
In my cupboards - in my bed
Touching my things;
Then with my food well fed.
I saw something that time
Through the kitchen and just by
The golden dried flowers that are not really mine,
But the wind howls strong around these trees
So maybe it was just
Some old fallen leaves.

A shiver runs over my face as the skies
Begin to grow heavy with winter snow
And my horse is restless while he tries to graze
For he too feels he is not alone.
Forever is a long time to share my home
With a shadow lost in a past life
Nobody's friend with nobody's wife:
So I will have to burn my beloved house down
To keep me safe and my horse from harm.
But as the last billow of smoke
Rises to the sky,
A cloak falls upon my shoulders
Whispering
The shadow is still
Alive.

BYE

The bright blue sparkling eyes
Lit up my room
And I was so surprised
I clung to fragile hope
But you just led me on...
I thought that we were friends again
But soon out of my dream
You were gone,
Out of my dream,
Out of my life
Into the cold steely night.
And all the memories
Side by side
Are hidden in a place
Where your angel cried
When the thunder rolled
One dark day:
Our friendship and our love
Forever blown away.

MY CASTLE ON A CLOUD

Come with me to my castle
Not very far away
It has been a lonely place
But I will change things today.
Come with me to my castle
The sun shines strong you see;
I can tread the steps with you
And you can dance with me.
I'll hold your hand
If you're afraid
The climb is high
For my castle is on cloud
My castle is in the sky.

Come with me to my castle
I can be a friend to you there
I can feel my body swaying
Not motionless in a chair.
Come with me to my castle
We can forget real life
For a while
I can pretend that everything is alright
You can look at me and smile.

Come with me to my castle
Where the past will fade away
The tears and crying will be somewhere else
My friend back to stay.
I can invite anyone I like
To my castle
And they won't even know
For the castle is in the clouds of my mind
Somewhere for me to go.

CAN SHE...?

Can she love you
like I love you
Can she hold you
stroke your hair
Can she love you
like I love you
Even when you are not there
Can she hold you
like I want to
Days and nights to share
Can she love you
like I love you
Just to take care
Can she love you
like I love you
When all the world
screams and shouts
Can she love you
like I love you
Can she be your friend
today
Can she love you
like I love you
Can she
stay away...?

FOR ALL TO LEAVE MY HOME

A quiet time for me to savour,
Sighs of relief from all four walls
And the pain that's there to remind me
Seems to subside
To no pain at all.

When all the strangers leave my home,
At last
I can be alone,
But the cold and damp
Saturday afternoon
Haunts me, taunts me,
Begs me to do
All those things I used to;
But I dare not look,
I cannot go,
For I can't walk
And did I know
The trees whisper so very slow
"He's never ever coming home."

But I can dream what I need to do,
Lay the table with his
Favourite food;
Let the wine breathe in a nice warm room,
Be here when he's cold and hungry
Like I used to do.

When all the strangers leave my home
I don't need them anymore
I just need you
To ease my pain
To hold me in arms
That feel the same.

The dream now ends
The strangers return
But one will always stay away.

I USED TO HAVE A FRIEND

Sweep me away so that I can't remember you.
The times I spent with my head
Locked in the clouds!
Now to face my own reality,
Wish my feet could touch the ground.
I used to have a friend
Some long time.

And the pictures all begin to fade
As I hear a long lost voice
Asking me to be brave,
But sometimes the loneliness creeps up on me
All the things I ever held dear
Slip gently away.
I used to have a friend
To love and hold me near.

When all the fickle laughter is over
And sleep is supposed to be,
I want to reach out for my friend
But in darkness I can't see;
And I wonder if in a hundred years
I'll still miss my friend
As much as the life I have
Is still missing me.

WILL I SEE YOU...?

She asked if she would
see him again,
And he said yes
But he did not know where or when:
She was not worried
This was déja-vu
She'd met him before
But he never knew...

She rose from the water
Her flawless aching body naked and brown,
He never seemed to notice
Although really he was charmed.
He said he would share her heartbreak
And bring her to his bed
Secretly she longed to hold him
But then she never said.
She remembered his golden hair
From long time ago:
His aching body stood strong
Not threatening, in any way
And she knew that they would love
And he knew it would be today.

He asked her what she wanted;
She did not know.
Fresh love for her
Would have to grow:
He was not worried
This was déja-vu
He'd met her before
But she never knew...

STILL TO SEE...

The haze of colours parade out on to the track,
Gleaming coats of finely tuned athletes shine in the winter sun.
Canter past... limber up...
Jockeys poised neatly upon their back
And I push my collar around my neck so the chilly wind cannot attack.
I've lost some of my life... I know I will never find
But as I look over towards the old Cleeve Hill ranging high above
I thank the Lord I am not blind...
Still to see the things I love.

I know how you feel as the horses' hooves touch the Cheltenham grass
And in anticipation your heart flutters
Like mine did in the past.
Now all the autumn leaves scatter in rustic brown and green
The winning post is in sight
You are still at the two mile start and I'm still in a dream.
Then the roar of the crowd from the last to the line
And the cheering ovation that brings a tear to someone's eye,
I watch the triumphant return
And thank the Lord I am not blind.

I savour some moments sometimes lost in the crowd
My friend you only said a brief hello
But I understand that things change... and it hurts... I know
Then another with compassionate smile turning to stone now
But only for a while.
The face is brave and why shouldn't it be!
The roars of applause I heard were once for me,
Then as the last ounce is given through steaming nostrils and sweat
With no fatal casualties then we've all won the bet.
Even in dusk you could paint a picture so fine
Where the glory and tears lay side by side
I look across the track just a shadow now ranges above
I thank the Lord I am not blind...
Still to see the things I love.

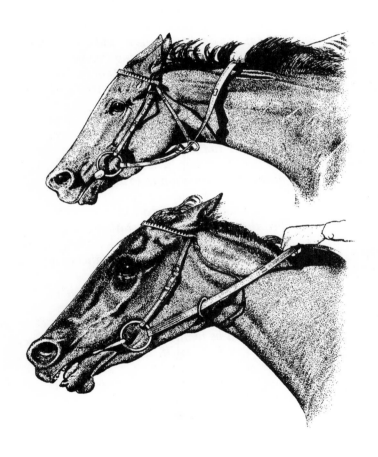

STATION TO STATION

Living... not waiting or watching
Another junction came,
And in my blindness I stepped out
Made people cry with pain
Never to walk again.
And the stations are filled with so many
Different people now
And the junctions come up so fast.
Sometimes there is so much confusion
As present mixes in with the past,
And I try so hard to be the divider
But sometimes I find myself asking "why?"
As I sit alone in a disused station
Where the trains keep passing me by.
I recognise the happy faces
My friends;
Celebrating, drinking champagne,
And I wave to them to wait for me
Then my life will be back the same,
But now their destination is so different
To mine
And I smile as they drift by.
Then the next train in the station
With new faces that I know:
They shout and beckon for me to join them
Alas I cannot go.
Less confused now at my decisions
Where fate gave me the choice
Of all the stations and all the junctions
Some will be wrong and some
Will be right.

WANT

I want you to cry and be sorry
I want you to hurt like I do
I want your heart to twinge
With sadness
When my name is mentioned
To you.
I want you to wake in the night
I want you to feel my pain
I want you to see me fight
Pray for me to get on my feet again.
I want you to forever know
It's not bitterness why I cry
I just miss my friend so very much
Sometimes I think I'll die.
I want you to be smiling
But never forget the tears
I want you always to remember
The love - the times - the years.
I want you to be angry
I feel so lonely now
And I want your face just to be
A stranger in the crowd.
I want my love for you
To be destroyed,
All memories to fade away
Lost and declared void.
I want you to know I love someone else
And my friend
I think he loves me too.
I want you to know
I'm happy
Even though I have to live
Without you.

WINTER RACING

Winter sky hangs heavy with cloud,
Dark dank day,
But still here we find a crowd
Muffled and scarved to keep out the cold.
Winter racing
Only for the brave and bold
And the charge.. fit and ready to do battle again.
Willing to please, never knowing the end,
Stands in serenity
Against darkened skies;
Not knowing if they will win, live or die.
This passion we possess
And fire into life
Makes us lift our heads
When they should be bloody and bowed!
Then not for us that we shed a tear
But the faller that still lays on the ground.
Winter racing
The thrill of the chase,
Spectacular leaps enjoyed at fast pace,
Affinity between horse and man.
Precision and braveness
Rolled into one;
And we watch - on the edge - in the shade
While you revel in your glory
Totally unafraid.
Euphoric feeling you have and hold
Acknowledging your charge and his unconquerable soul.
Winter racing
The love of my life, as I wake
To galloping hooves in the dead of night.

HIS FOOTSTEPS NEVER FALTERED

He said he would have to go soon
Time was getting on,
He'd been with me all afternoon
And all afternoon I was strong.
We sat in the hospital ward
His face showed signs of strain,
As he bowed his head to the floor
Disguising his own felt pain.

The brace held my head and neck
Broken in the fall,
And this man who once had loved me
Became a stone built wall.
I wanted to reach out and touch him
But voice was all I had,
And now I felt it breaking
Wistful and aching sad.

I can't remember if he stroked my hair
Of if I was glad he came,
His footsteps never faltered
When I tried to call his name.
He didn't hear my voice
My call was in vain,
A veil of silence seemed to fall
As others shared my pain.

I couldn't turn to see him
I gasped for air to breathe,
Willing him to look back at me
Crying for him not to leave.
But his footsteps never faltered
He didn't hear me call,
Emotion tightened round my throat
And tears began to fall.

So there I sat in wretchedness
With no hope left at all,
His footsteps never faltered
But never again would I call.
Composed I'd be tomorrow
And deny I called his name,
His footsteps never faltered
Because he never came.

HELLO...

I remember things that haunt me now
So many things
So long ago.
I remember your face and how you made me feel
When you smiled and watched me on winter days,
And I... pretending
I didn't know...
Waited for you to say... Hello.
Then once we spoke and you will never know
How you made me feel that day,
After love had screamed
And turned away.
Someone to help me find myself again
A friendly face
A strong tall man.
Someone to notice I have a smile
And find me attractive
Upon the eye.
But sadly we waited far too long
Unsure... then time was gone.
The smiles and looks are over now,
But I'm sure that they were real
And for that time
You will never know
How good you made me feel.

LOOKING FOR SUMMER

We held hands and walked to the sea
Looking for summer
In those old days when you were loving me
We laughed and screamed to the crashing
Of the waves
And lay on warm sand
Hazy loving days.
Now everytime that cold day folds
Everytime I see your face
Photo, picture on my wall,
Everytime that north wind blows,
Hazy days come back to me.
You kissed my tears
When I was lost in the rain
But looking for summer now
Will never be the same.

I danced a dance I will never tread again
Looking for summer,
Was never going to end.
We laughed and loved 'till
Early morning came
And then we laughed and loved
To do it all again.
Now everytime that cold day folds
Every day I see your face
Gone forever summer days.
Just left with winter place.

✣✣✣✣

THE TEAR THAT ESCAPES ME...

Love so deep it tore my soul
And it cut both ways
'Till there was nothing at all,
But I found a strength
From deep within
And I smiled one night
For all to see
But now alone
The tear escapes me...

Dark so dark and quiet now
Frivolity and laughter moved on.
And the time that is gone
Leaves me with a wanton taste
So many things to do
So many things to be
I lay in solitude
And then
The tear escapes me...

The deep pain that deep ache
Seems to subside a little
As time goes by,
But my heart keeps reminding me
Every single day
That the love I felt
Will never ever go away
And it's when I want to be free
The tear escapes me...

FREEDOM

Feeling kind of restless
When old freedom calls my name:
It whispers through the doorways
"Please come with me to play
We can follow a road to nowhere
Where a winding river flows with dreams."
And I move towards the window,
So close to freedom now:
It stands upon the green grass
Nonchalantly leans against the wall,
Freedom holds out its hand to me
I feel the sun again
I taste the food of hope
As freedom beckons me to run.
And I turn to run - forever to be free
But face my jailer
Who has thrown away the key.

More sleepless nights
Where only freedom calls my name
And the memories of the sea
Sound of crashing waves.
Freedom's gone forever
And it won't be coming back this way.
I've missed the road to nowhere
And the river that flows with dreams.
In my loss, trying to gain,
I had to kiss goodbye to freedom.
But I won't live behind a door,
And my voice can still be heard
As I fight for
My freedom... my freedom
Like before.

FROM MY WINDOW

The sun was bright though the day was cool
And from my window
I could almost touch the view,
The leaves beginning to turn
In different shades of autumn,
And a blue sky herding fluffy white clouds
As if it had just caught them.
My horse grazing happily on field of green:
I wished I could paint a picture
For all to see
Before the day folds into night time
And darkness covers me.

I turn back the page
But my life is not there
Today I feel lost
And no one seems to care.
From my window
I can see
Laughing smiling faces
But they are oblivious
To me.

The sun now gone and sky turns grey,
From my window
I watch you ride my horse
I can't hold the reins anymore
Only feeling his contact when he nuzzles my face;
Silent rapport.
Still; I smile to know I've had the same
Now you can feel something
That once was mine,
Something I had back in time.

FOR THE HOUSE ON THE HILL

I hope, forever you will stay warm
Against the chill of the wind,
Standing so tall your strength
And aura the first thing I see;
But I can see beneath the structure
Beneath the solid beams
I can see the hand of thoughtfulness
Playing on the breeze.

Embraced, I felt as in your door
I reaped rewards of comfort
For a house only needs one person to breathe
A life to share peaceful moments.
As far as an eye can see
Of a view that will never tire
Your ever changing scenery
That comes with different seasons to admire.

Inside and outside the ambience
Touches as you leave:
That's the hand of thoughtfulness
Playing on the breeze.

CLUTCHING ON TO THE NIGHT

Clutching on to the night
With furtive hands
I embrace my friends... hope they will understand.
My need to live
Far greater now
Since fate decided
Where and how.
Every minute of life
So precious to me
This kind of future I didn't forsee.
I embrace my friends... willing them to understand.
As I clutch on to the night
With desperately furtive hands,
Hoping these times will never end
While wishing for the sun to stay down
And the night to rage with
Sight and sound.
I embrace my friends... knowing they will understand...

PRISONER
OF MY LOVE

Lying in the solitude of night
Embraced by love and care
Stretched out with freedom
Entwined in pleasure;
Birds sing dawn chorus
The end is never
Then broken hearted
The end is now.

I don't know which way to turn
I've never been this lonely.
Then you come along
To be my lover again.
You fill my nights by loving me
Spinning my head around
Leaving by morning so slowly
While I try so hard
To hang on to my dream.
You've never been there for me
Already left the scene.
And I know deep down
You can never want me.

Look into my eyes
Sometimes he does
And what about the way
I sometimes look at him.
We laugh together and then I know
I want you both
But have to let go;
So diffidently I see
All of us love
But we can't love me.

PRETEND

I promised not to write you - but then I find me weak.
The sickness in my stomach
Wakes me from my sleep
And I'm tired of pretending
I don't need you anymore.
If only I could see you
Hold you like before.
I promised not to look - at your picture on the wall,
But I miss you and I hate you
And I love you most of all.
I'm tired of pretending
I feel no need to cry
Cold takes me every night
No one - next to me - to lie
I promised you your freedom - and then I promised me mine
But I didn't know your freedom meant
For me this jail of time.
So how brave would I have to be
To face your face again?
So you can promise not to haunt me
And free me from
Pretend.

THE RINKY DINKY BOAT

Skies were blue that summer's day
As I set ready to sail away;
Wind blew softly through my hair
As I floated gently on the sea
Just rinky dinky boat
And me.
Only one seagull in the sky
Soaring, weaving, duck and dive
Sea just splashing, lapping low
A sound some never know.
Sun suspended high in air,
Glinted reflections everywhere.
No soul for miles can I see
Just rinky dinky boat
And me.
I close my eyes to feel the sway
And the warmth of the sun
On my face plays.
Tickling sometimes for the breeze
Feels like fingers
Aching to tease;
But for miles and miles now on the sea
Just rinky dinky boat
And me.
I never want to end this time
Though the sun begins to fall
Out of the sky,
But the land has loudest cry
In the middle of the green, black sea
Alone, I could die.
This feeling soon will only be mine
The sway of my boat
On an outgoing tide,
Sounds of sea lapping and gulls that sigh
Tickling fingers aching to tease
Camouflaged as summer breeze.
The sun kisses and drops upon horizon
As I touch land,
And my feet feel the still warm golden sand.
I sit awhile looking out to a moonlit sea.
The day has ended for
Rinky dinky boat
And me.

THE LAST FLING

Clouds began to gather and now it was bitterly cold
Most people including me missing the last race
To make our journey home.
The traffic was building up and headlights were shining bright.
As we left Cleeve Hill behind us
Alone to face the night.
And I looked across one last time to view the awesome land
But instead I could only see a fallen jockey
Still with bridle in hand.
The figure dressed now in muddy silks
Had smiled broadly earlier on;
But now his face was ashen with pain and cold
From meeting that fence all so wrong.
He held his back as if it would break
The glory for today now gone.
My pleasure subsided for a while
But he said he was okay.
Only I can realise - the false faint trace - of his smile
Immersed in pain and for now, taken away.
And I was glad that I will never fall
On the cold turf again that way.
Then a sadness hit me knowing it wouldn't last
To the end of the day.
By tomorrow when the soreness and bruising begins to fade away
The thirst and hunger for winners,
Will be back with a vengeance begging you to play;
The magic never leaves you - for anything - even after
The Last Fling.

RIDE AWAY

Watch you ride round and round
Horse and rider now as one
Floating gently over sands - reins of leather - held in velvet hands
Walk - then into canter - slow
Reins of contact telling steed how to go
Jodhpured leg and heels to squeeze
While the big leafy boughs of two nearby trees
Bounce and sway - summer breeze
And the house that is there
Amongst the leaves - hidden now - until winter siege
Sky laden with rich white cloud
Trying to pretend - to me
That it is really - thick cold ice - covering a deep blue sea
But warm friendly sun keeps peaking through
Making steed's coat shine - a day that makes the living fine
And hung on stable ends
Hay racks bloom with flower - barrels and baskets brim over
In sight - with wonderful colour
Watching time now over
Memories of yesterday - horse and rider - still as one
Ready to ride away.

❖❖❖❖

106

MY DAY - MY NIGHT - MY REAL TRUE LIFE

MY DAY

Don't see you for ages
You're just a friend to me:
I see that you are handsome
With friendly smiling eyes,
But brown haired, blue eyed boy
When you talk to me
No one is surprised.
Even though we laugh together
No romance they will see
For you can only ever be
A passing friend to me.

MY NIGHT

My arms they ache so much
From holding - loving you:
And I melt under your tender touch
Your presence warms me through,
And why after all this time
Do you tell me that you care?
Why do you want me to hold you
Say I will always be there.
Then I wake to morning light
And reality is so unfair.

MY REAL TRUE LIFE

I'm no fool - I don't pretend
I know where danger lies
And I would never dare to think
No matter how loud my heart
Cries.

CONCEALED SPACE OF ME

Dark clouds gather round the concealed space of me,
The air grows ever colder
As the sky becomes a murkier sea.
And I still try to give, yet it's hard to believe
For I'm torn for the loss of a lover - and the life
I had to leave.
I'm living within the concealed space of me,
Hurting and fooling you all the time:
All you know is what you see.

The rain lashes down trying to wash away the pain,
But I don't need to sleep with you
Even as my heart grows heavy
And starry moments make me think
I do.
You can't come into this concealed space of mine
Within its cave - only I can survive.

All you know is what you hear and see,
Hurting and fooling all the time.
I'm living within a tranquil space of me
Somewhere beautiful - lovers and life never leave
Between the clear blue sea - and forever sunny sky
On the avenue where darkness shines:
Concealed space of mine.

BEFORE YOU LEAVE

Good to know there is someone
For me to fool around.
I like to make you laugh
Even when sometimes I'm feeling down
And I like it when you say
"You just think you're so funny today"
And it's nice having you around the place
For a short stay.
My home a place of peacefulness
Where sanctuary can be found
And then ablaze with laughter
Uncontrollable - profound.
Then that creeping feel of envy
Stands next to freedom's friend
But only for a second
And then we are laughing again.

So

Stroke my hair before you leave
Kiss my lips - but not passionately
Then I can always be a friend to you
And you - a friend to me.

NOTHING REMAINS THE SAME

If only that special time
Could last forever - being kind
When love was enriched
With fortune and fame,
But sadly for us
Nothing remains the same.

So we look ahead - into the dark
No guiding light to make a fresh start
And we look back - with pleading eyes
If only for that special time;
But no one else made us play the game
And now for us
Some things are not the same.

So what to do but catch hold of life,
Proud to have special memories
Locked away in the dead of night;
So much to do and see and say
For you and me a different day.
So we grow and strengthen - happy to know
We are not shallow people
Nor hollow.

We've tasted the glory
And played the game:
So lucky! - for our passion
Will always remain the same.

EMOTIONALLY CHARGED

At seventeen emotion was either girl or lad
When a pretty face could turn your head
And so often wanted to share
Your bed.
Then as you grow emotion falls in step
Greater then and with more depth.
People enter and leave your life
Sometimes with love
Some with strife.
With different times to touch your heart

You are - emotionally charged

Emotion - this feeling that often approaches - slow
Starts in your stomach - staying there for days
As a knot - deep and low.
You hope the sickness you feel won't show
But your face - sometimes too easily - gives way,
Breaking into a smile or a cry,
A laugh or a sigh.
Inside and out it can tear your world apart
Before stealthily making progress
To rest behind your bosom - hide beneath your heart

I am - emotionally charged

Emotion - your head takes over - now
Keep relaxed and calm
Before it creeps and reaches - to your throat
Where it tightens
A strangle hold of sadness - shallow and ashen - thin and cold
Nowhere to run, nowhere to hide,
Big eyes defenceless - for reason or none - you cry.
In happiness too many words flow
Cheeks flush, eyes shine bright,
You're visibly lifted when love - is home at night:

We are - emotionally charged

112

THE LOVE OF YOUR LIFE
(SHEBA)

You said
"She is the love of my life"
And I knew it wasn't me.
She looked at you with adoring eyes
Always faithful
She would be.
Her silky black coat did shine
As she bounded to and fro
And her special trick of staying still
Was when you placed a chocolate
On her nose.
She would have waited forever
For your command - to toss it in the air
Catching it so precisely
She loved you - and she cared.

Sheba
Was the love of you're life
And you were certainly hers.
Memories for you to treasure
For the rest of your years.

❖❖❖❖

FROM MY WINDOW
CHANGING SEASONS

From my window now the scene is bleak and bare
The field ravaged by winter snow
Has left a mass of sludge
And only little hope
For the grass to grow.

And further away across the land
The variety of trees stand naked and tall,
Stripped of leaves by the wind and the rain
That were bestowed on them
As winter came.

They stand their ground against the grey old sky
Waiting patiently for spring
Then summer to arrive.
When suddenly without warning the buds will appear
And before the migrating birds come home
The thick green leaves to cover the bareness is here.

Soon my view will be a sunny haze
And I'll look towards the trees
As they magically hold my gaze.
Then as the summer comes to its end
They will burst into wonderful colour again.

Like the model showing her finest clothes
All different shades of colour grows.
Then one by one the leaves will dry and fall
The birds will leave for their warmer home,
And we'll be waiting naked in the wind and rain
Just like before - when winter came.

I'M IN YOUR SLEEP...

Don't feel afraid of the coolness of the breeze
that glides over your handsome face
Aching to please
It's only me
In your room
In your sleep
Then
Into your bed
I creep
Underneath your covers
In between your sheets
I'm with you now
As you sleep.

Don't feel afraid of the warmth of the breeze
that glides over your naked body
Aching to please
It's only me
In your dream
In your sleep
Then
In your love
I keep
Pull away your covers
Slide off your sheets
I'm with you now
As you sleep.

Don't be afraid of the silence of the breeze
that glides over your contentment
As I leave
It's only me
In your dream
In your sleep
Then
In your wake
You seek
Perfume on your covers
Scent on your sheets
You're alone now
I'm only in your sleep.

OCEAN CLOTHES...

Saw me dancing by the ocean
Playing with the waves
My body only just covered
In pale diaphanous clothes.
I saw you and you froze
But like the moon that shines so brightly
And the stars that never fade
You can always watch me dancing
Never be afraid.

Saw me talking to the ocean
Laughing with the waves
Laid upon the warm sand.
Silently I prayed
I was hoping that you loved me
Then I saw you and you froze
Even though the night was warm and wondrous
And I wore pale diaphanous clothes.

Saw me swimming in the ocean
Like a mermaid unafraid
Did you hear me whispering
Calling out your name.
Or was it just the sound
Of the wild crashing waves
That brought you to my shore
In control and unafraid.

Saw you standing by the ocean
And suddenly I froze
You whispered that you loved me
And from the water I rose.
See our eyes sparkle like diamonds
And the moon and stars just froze
With the night now warm and wondrous
I discarded my pale diaphanous clothes.

PAINT ME A PICTURE
AND
I'LL WRITE YOU A POEM

Paint me a landscape with a colourful
Sky
A scene of our friendship
That will never die.
Time passes so quickly
A decade has gone by
Where we revelled in our sadness
Then didn't even cry.
So smile for our friendship
When you see a colourful
Sky.

Many thing have changed
In our hearts and with our minds;
Travel away to your highlands
But never forget the times,
When you laughed and you were happy
With old friends by your side.

Paint me a landscape with a colourful
Sky
And I'll write you a poem
Of mine.
Place it somewhere
Facing a window so it can see
The colourful sky of
Friendship
That looks down on
You and me.

I CAN'T EXPLAIN

I see myself locked in a mirror dream
Sweeping up the crinkly,
Burnt orange leaves.
No tears... A strong figure
Dressed in rustic brown,
And I lend the girl some money
Then the bus rushes off
Not making a sound.
As I sweep up the fallen autumn leaves
Two loose horses gallop by
And a lady raises her hand
But I tell her
They are not mine.

I'm there with a friend and look straight at you
A solemn face that sees
Right through,
And your face so clear you begin to smile
At me,
But your words are carried away
As I walk by.
I don't talk to you and I don't see.
In rustic brown I'm dressed
And you are just a stranger to me.

My new friend we hug and kiss,
He loves me dearly
But I only love him a bit;
He reaches out for me just to take care
And I want to love him
But my love is elsewhere.

❖❖❖❖

118

LOST YOUTH... BUT WISER WOMEN

Lost youth for us now my friends,
But wiser women are we
With treasured memories
We will never let go.
Our paths once together
Woven so differently,
So nearly losing touch for a time.
But we have fought with adversity
And the ambience around us still shines
Lost youth - maybe
But wiser women are we.

And I look at you,
The person I once knew,
Remembering sparkling eyes
So many of your ways remain the same
Now you can smile - where once you cried.
Lost youth - maybe
But wiser women are we.

And I look at you
Remembering your laughter,
Fun in our younger days
Even through many tears
Now you can smile
Where once you had pain.
Lost youth - maybe
But wiser women are we.

And I look at me
Such a different person I see
No more dancing till early morn;
So I focus my life
Away from love and strife
My heart nevermore to be torn
Lost youth - maybe
But wiser women are we.

Lost youth - maybe - now my friends,
But the rest of our lives
To savour.
Our strength is found with courage and wisdom
For all to see
And of course
Wiser women are we.

WHEN YOU'RE NOT HERE

Locked together in warm embrace
Strong arms around me keeping me safe.
Holding on you're loving me
And it feels so real
It feels so right
I kiss you only to realise
Another dream on another night.
And why do you say you love me
When you see me this way
I can only hope
I don't confuse my nights
With your days.

Then you're not here
And I feel I'm missing you
As daylight turns into nightfall,
And together we dance
In candlelight
Only you're not there at all.
And the laughter we share leaves a smile on my face
That turns into a frown,
As the day breaks into
My nightime dream
So I can't hold you
Anymore.

TEMPTATION...

Don't tell me that you love me
Don't look at me that way
You know I am not free
And we can never run away.

But whenever I see you
I'm led into temptation
And
I don't know for certain
Which way to turn.

Don't tell me that you need me
Don't look into my eyes
You open out your arms
My feelings I disguise.

But whenever I'm near you
I'm led into temptation
And
I know for certain
The hurt will rebel.

Don't take me to your bed
Don't ask me to stay
For the guilty get no sleep
At the break of day.

But what about my friend I vowed to trust?
You lead me into temptation
And
I don't know for certain
If it's love or just simply lust.

THE PRICE OF BEING
RECKLESS

Plays heavy on my mind now - the things that were said
And done.
I thought our love would last forever
Never thought he would come along.
Making my heart flutter - filling me with desire
Like you used to do;
Some long time when our love was one fiery soul.
And I want to take you - shake you - tell you something's wrong!
But we avoid the issue
And just carry on.
I watch you - waiting - till you're out of sight,
Then I tear myself inside out.
Where does wrong start to become right!
I reach for the telephone - I need to hear his voice,
He tells me that he loves me
So I have to make the choice,
And I know I'm going to hurt you - tear your life apart.
The price of being reckless
With my love and lust;
Leaves you with a broken heart
No one left to trust.
My love suspended in limbo - can I stay? - should I go?
I look around our house - our home - our togetherness.
Why do I feel so alone?
When the laughter is ingrained in the walls,
Where the warmth lives in every room.
You will be home - I must tell you soon.
I'm sorry but all these things will be gone;
They will turn cold and blue.
That is how you will feel - when I leave you.
The tears will soon run dry
And the hurt will disappear.
I tear myself inside out - for I'm alone tonight
Wondering when wrong starts to become right.
He told me that he loved me - I had to make the choice.
The price of being reckless
I never heard that in his voice...

UNDYING LOVE

I've had some times to remember...
Until forever
I've waited for this day,
To wear a simple ivory dress
In the church to pray.
Scooped neck with arms that from elbow flare,
Fresh wild flowers arranged gently
In long curly hair,
Feet caressed in satin shoes
Today I win my love for you.
Love that through darkened day
I have never given away
The silence of valour in the sky,
I'm ready to wed
The man for whom I would surely die.

And as quiet chaos invades my home
I feel I'm now without care;
For dressed in black and grey
You will be there
Waiting for me in my splendour to arrive
Underneath the sunniest of all skies.

Two metallic chestnut horses
With blaze of white down their foreheads;
Manes plaited or flowing long
Drive me away towards the sun.
Harness soaped, buckles gleam
Carriage caught in sunlight scene
Shining like gold from fabled tale
Horses pacing, striding proud
Steel clad hooves clattering loud.
Wheels spin in perfect motion
Down the winding riverside road
Where the spangled water of dream flows.
Saying goodbye as I pass this way
Leaving all behind me now as with you
I will promise to stay.

Slowly, carefully horses come to halt
To deliver me into outstretched arms.
In a simple straw-lined wooden box
No satin or silk for me to lie.
I lived. I loved.
So for you there is no need to cry.

My arms, as asked, crossed over my chest
Still holding on to bereft heart
That hid beneath my breast
Finding a safe place to rest
Amid life's turmoil of love's unruliness.
So with trees in bloom and birds to sing
Horses grazing in pastures green
Mares and foals frolicking.
The summer rife with beauty and desire
Let me glide into the eternal fire,
Fresh flowers in my hair
Simple ivory dress to wear
Flowers surrounding body fair
A soul left resting upon the air.

❖❖❖❖

TIMELESS
(For Trevor Rees-Jones)

Timeless; it must seem to be
Lying alone wondering if this is true
Or just a wicked dream.
And we wait; our day and night embroiled
With circumstance and you,
For whom we care.
For the pain - with you - to bear.
Waiting for news from distant place
Wanting only truth
Spoken with honest face...

Timeless; now you must be strong
From this day to reverse your role
For however long.
And we wait; in your day and night
Finding the right words to say,
For you we pray.
The anguish - in your soul - to leave.
Waiting for news from distant land
Wanting only truth
Written by honest hand...

Timeless; life for valiant man
Caught up in someone's destiny
Where fate dealt the hand.
And we wait; hoping for your day and night
To find some peace in rich sunlight,
Away from rain.
Special love - for you - to reap.
When you return from foreign part
With only truth
In honest heart...

COMFORT YOU...

Let me cover your face with kisses
Stay with me awhile,
Let me drive away your demons
And you can drive away mine.
Let me stroke your aching brow
They don't need to know,
Let me be your hideaway
Somewhere safe for you to go.
Let me share your silence
If you need me to,
Let me be the one - the one
To comfort you.

Let me cover you with warmth
In your sleepless night,
Let me hold on to you gently
And you can hold me tight.
Let me be your shoulder
If you feel the need to cry,
Let me be your sanctuary
'Till you're strong enough to fly.
Let me be your protection
If you need me to,
Let me be the one - the one
To comfort you.

Let me cover you with magic
In your hours of need,
Let me be your haven
Until you feel free.
Let me be your light
When darkness seems to prevail,
Let me be your guide
When everything seems to fail.
Let me be your answer
If you want me to,
Let me be the one - the one
To comfort you.

❖❖❖❖

NIL DESPERANDUM
(Never Despair)

When days are dark and nights are long
While you have life
You must be strong;
Nil Desperandum
Never despair
For your life is precious
But only if for yourself
You care.

When Summer sleeps and Autumn cries
Of its wondrous beauty
For our eyes
Then we can conquer, battle and fight;
Nil Desperandum
Never despair
Meet the challenge
But only if for yourself
You care.

When days are bright and nights are warm
And you're waiting for a new day to dawn
With strength you found deep inside
Searching over - no need to hide
Nil Desperandum
Never despair
You defended your honour
And only if for yourself
You care.